W9-AAZ-165

DATE DUE			

158.1
AND

33577000617603
Andrews, Linda
Wasmer.

Meditation

KANELAND HIGH SCHOOL LIBRARY
MAPLE PARK, IL   60151

400859 01538   24114B   038

Meditation

Linda Wasmer Andrews

Kaneland High School Library
47 W326 Keslinger Road
Maple Park, IL 60151

Franklin Watts
A Division of Scholastic Inc.
New York • Toronto • London • Auckland • Sydney
Mexico City • New Delhi • Hong Kong
Danbury, Connecticut

158.1
AND

33577000617603

Dedication

For David, Amanda, and Michael,
who are filled with lovingkindness.

Cover design by Robert O'Brien.
Interior design by Kathleen Santini.
Illustrations by Patricia Rasch.

Library of Congress Cataloging-in-Publication Data

Andrews, Linda Wasmer.
    Meditation / Linda Wasmer Andrews.
        p. cm. — (Life balance)
Summary: Explains popular methods of meditation such as zen,
transcendental meditation, and yoga and discusses their effects
on stress and general mental health.
Includes bibliographical references and index.
    ISBN 0-531-12219-0 (lib. bdg.)   0-531-16609-0 (pbk.)
    1. Meditation—Juvenile literature. 2. Meditation I. Title. II. Series.
    BF637.M4 A53 2003
    158.1'2—dc22
                                          2003007153

Copyright © 2004 by Scholastic Inc.
All rights reserved. Published simultaneously in Canada.
Printed in the United States of America.
1 2 3 4 5 6 7 8 9 10 R 13 12 11 10 09 08 07 06 05 04

Table of Contents

Meditation
Myth Busters

Marie is sitting on the floor. Her legs are crossed, her back is straight, and her eyes are closed. She is breathing deeply and regularly. With each breath out, she chants something that sounds like "ohmmm." A peaceful half smile is on her face.

Josh is walking through the park. He is moving at his usual pace. His breathing seems to be keeping time with his steps. First, he takes a long breath in for four steps. Then, he lets a long breath out for four steps. His whole body looks relaxed.

Ginny is eating an orange at the kitchen table. She seems wrapped up in what she is doing. First, she spends a few moments looking at the whole fruit and rolling it around in her hands. Then, she carefully peels and sections the orange. When she is finished, she lifts a section to her nose, closes her eyes, and breathes in deeply. Finally, she begins to eat the orange very slowly. She seems to be enjoying every single bite.

What do these teenagers have in common? Each is meditating in the way that suits that person best. Many people believe there is only one way to meditate, but actually there are several. There are ways to suit people who are usually calm and quiet, but there also are ways to suit those who have trouble sitting still and are always on the go. In fact, students with busy, stressful lives stand to gain the most from the relaxing effects of meditation.

Some people think that meditation is difficult or mysterious yet it can be as simple and natural as focusing your attention on a word, your breathing, or your eating. Meditation is nothing more than the practice of focusing your mind on a particular thing or activity. Some forms of it can be done by just about anyone, anywhere, anytime.

Meditation is nothing more than the practice of focusing your mind on a particular thing or activity. Some forms of it can be done by just about anyone, anywhere, anytime.

....

What Meditation Isn't

Meditation relaxes your body and calms your mind. Not every relaxing activity is meditation, however—only the ones in which you focus your attention. It's like taking a laser pointer and shining it on one particular thing or activity. All your attention is concentrated on that one tiny spot. Listening to music while you intently focus on the sounds themselves and let go of other distracting thoughts and daydreams is meditation. Listening to music while you do your homework, think about your plans for the weekend, and daydream about becoming a rap star isn't.

Myths and Truths

There are many false ideas about meditation. Some myths have been repeated so often that people start to believe they are true. Here are some of the most common ones.

Myth: You have to be a little flaky to meditate.

Truth: All kinds of people are drawn to meditation. This includes many teenagers and children as well as adults. Successful people in a wide range of jobs practice meditation. Famous figures who say they have meditated at some point in their lives include film director Oliver Stone, actress Gwyneth Paltrow, singer Madonna, professional golfer Tiger Woods, poet Robert Pinsky, and former vice president Al Gore.

Quiet Brain, Calm Mind

Meditation is an ancient practice. Only recently, however, have scientists begun using high-tech tools to study exactly what happens inside the brain during meditation. In one study, scientists at the University of Pennsylvania hooked up meditators to devices containing a special dye. Each meditator was also given one end of a long string; the other end was tied to a researcher's finger. As the researcher waited, the person practiced meditation. When the meditator felt most deeply relaxed, he or she tugged on the string. The researcher, feeling this signal, released dye into the person's arm. The dye traveled through the person's bloodstream to the brain. The researcher then took special pictures of the brain, and the dye showed which areas had the greatest blood flow. These parts of the brain were considered to be most active at that time.

This study showed that the brain doesn't completely turn off during meditation. However, it does seem to shut out information that it might normally let in. Other scientists have found similar effects from meditation. Their findings show that meditation may calm the mind by quieting the brain. For example:

• Reticular formation—This network of nerve cells controls consciousness and arousal. It receives incoming information and puts the brain on alert if needed. During meditation, arousal signals are muted.

• Thalamus—This part of the brain relays information from the senses to other areas deep inside the brain. It acts as a gatekeeper, sending some signals and stopping others from going any farther. During meditation, the flow of incoming information from the senses is slowed to a trickle.

• Parietal lobe—This part of the brain processes information from the senses about the outside world. It helps you locate yourself in time and space. During meditation, activity in the parietal lobe slows down.

• Frontal lobe—This part of the brain is responsible for the highest-level mental functions. It is involved in thinking, decision-making, and planning. During meditation, the frontal lobe is much less active.

• Limbic system—This group of brain structures plays a key role in emotion and memory. It also helps regulate heart rate and breathing rate. Unlike most parts of the brain, blood flow here actually increases during meditation.

Myth: You have to be a religious person to meditate.

Truth: Meditation doesn't have to involve religion. It's true that most of the great religions of the world include some practices that can be used for meditation. Also, many people turn to meditation for spiritual reasons. However, others are interested strictly in the health benefits. Meditation is a great way to relieve stress. This, in turn, can improve your overall emotional and physical health. Among other things, it can reduce anxiety, decrease depression, and lower high blood pressure.

Myth: Adults are the only ones faced with real stress.

Truth: Adults may believe this, but teenagers know differently. Some teens worry about their grades or have trouble making friends at school. Others brood over family problems or have trouble getting along at home. Still others live in areas where violence, drugs, and gangs are common. Factors such as these add up to an overdose of stress. Meditation is one of the best ways to ease that stressed-out feeling.

Myth: Meditation isn't relevant to the real world.

Truth: Meditation can be a powerful tool for personal change. People who practice meditation can learn to harness this power. They can then use it to work toward real-world goals. Consider, for example, the Falun Gong group, which sprang up in China in the 1990s. It teaches meditation as a means of achieving better physical and spiritual well-being. The group now has tens of millions of members.

In 1999, ten thousand Falun Gong followers gathered outside government buildings in Beijing, the capital of China. The daylong demonstration was peaceful. People just stood silently or meditated. The Chinese government, however, saw the popularity of the group as a threat. Soon afterward, it banned the group. The Chinese government seemed to be worried that these individual meditators might band together to become a force for social change.

Myth: Meditation is (yawn) boring.

Truth: Many people feel some boredom or restlessness when they first start to meditate. Most are surprised, though, by how quickly these feelings vanish. It makes sense, when you think about it. Meditation is a way of focusing on your inner experience. What could be more fascinating to you than you!

The Secret to Success

Another common belief is that there must be some deep, dark secret to meditation. The only one who knows the secret, the thinking goes, is a wise, old man with a long, gray beard, who is sitting in a cave at the top of a mountain. You have to find the old man and convince him to share his secret if you want to learn how to meditate.

That's the myth. The truth is that you don't have to climb any mountains or find any caves. You don't even have to talk to any wise old men. The secret to successful meditation is much closer to home. All you have to do is look within yourself.

Try this exercise: Close your eyes for a few minutes, and notice what happens with your thoughts. Now open your eyes. Were you surprised by how busy your mind was? Your thoughts may have raced ahead to the test next period or the big game this weekend. They may have drifted back to a conversation you had with your best friend this morning or the TV show you watched last night. They may even have floated off on a daydream about your fantasy car or the cute student sitting next to you. One way or another, though, your mind was probably on the go.

All this thinking, thinking, thinking makes it hard to focus your attention on just one thing for more than a few seconds. To meditate, you need to become aware of your mind's activity so that you can slow it down. This involves observing your own thoughts, feelings, and sensations as they arise. That way, you can gently bring your attention back to the thing or activity you want to focus on. In short, the secret to successful meditation is self-awareness, the act of observing your own mind.

Meditation in Action

Meditation requires quieting your mind. This doesn't mean becoming too laid back and spaced out for school or other activities, however. Part of what meditation teaches you is to stay calm and concentrate intently. It also helps you connect with yourself, with what you are doing, or with other people. These abilities can then be applied to school, sports, or anything else you might want. In fact, you may be surprised by what you can accomplish once you have learned how to relax and stay focused.

Why Meditate?

At the Maharishi School in Fairfield, Iowa, the students practice Transcendental Meditation (TM). This is a form of meditation in which the person focuses on a special sound or word, which is repeated over and over. Here are some of the reasons that students there give for meditating:

"After I meditate, . . . I feel sharper, clearer, and altogether more happy. In sports, I have found that I can play much longer and above my skill level."—seventh-grade boy

"After I do my TM, I feel like I can do anything. I feel rested and ready to take on whatever the day throws my way."—eighth-grade girl

"Personally, I feel much more relaxed and less stressed throughout the day. I'm less tired and have an increased ability to concentrate and focus on my studies. Most important, I feel much more inner happiness."—tenth-grade boy

Test Your Self-Awareness

Your mind is constantly buzzing with thoughts, feelings, and sensations. How aware are you of what your own busy mind is up to? This short quiz can help you find out how self-aware you may already be.

1. When you try to concentrate, your attention is like:
    a. a laser pointer, shining on a tiny spot
    b. a flashlight, lighting up a narrow path
    c. a floodlight, lighting up everything in sight

2. When you feel stressed out, you usually react by:
    a. taking some time to relax and unwind
    b. ordering yourself to calm down
    c. developing a headache or stomachache

3. If you had to spend a whole day alone, you would:
    a. have a great time and enjoy the company
    b. be OK if you had a TV or CD player
    c. go nuts by the end of the day

4. If you tried to imagine a peaceful scene, you would:
    a. see, hear, and feel it vividly in your mind
    b. see it briefly in your mind before getting bored
    c. not waste your time on something so silly

5. If you saw a rainbow as you were walking home, you would:
    a. take a few moments to soak up its beauty
    b. think "that's pretty" as you hurried along
    c. barely notice—what's the big deal anyway?

6. If your mind were to behave like a monkey, it would be:
    a. lively but sometimes quiet when you wanted it to be
    b. either active or quiet—it's hard to predict which
    c. always chattering and jumping from branch to branch

Scoring

Give yourself 4 points for each "a" answer, 2 points for each "b," and 0 points for each "c." Then add up your points.

24 points: You're already meditating, aren't you? But keep reading anyway, because there is always more to learn about meditation.

16–23 points: You're fairly in tune with your own thoughts, feelings, and sensations. Meditation will help sharpen your self-awareness.

8–15 points: You're a bit out of touch with what's happening in your own mind. Meditation can help you get in touch with yourself.

0–7 points: Who is that person living in your body? Meditation can help you get to know yourself and learn to live a more relaxed life.

Basketball coach Phil Jackson explains how meditation works for athletes in his book *Sacred Hoops:* "Basketball is a complex dance . . . To excel, you need to act with a clear mind and be totally focused on what *everyone* on the floor is doing." Jackson meditates, and he has used the principles of meditation to guide players such as Michael Jordan, Shaquille O'Neal, and Dennis Rodman.

Athletes refer to the state of total focus on a game as being "in the zone." Psychologists use the term "flow" for the same state. The idea is that you get so wrapped up in whatever you are doing that you lose yourself completely in the activity. Time seems to stand still, and your senses spring to heightened alertness. You feel thrilled just to be doing whatever it is you are doing, whether it's running a race, writing a story, painting a picture, or simply gazing at a sunset.

In short, flow is the way you feel when you're having some of the best times of your life. Meditation helps prepare you for

The idea is that you get so wrapped up in whatever you are doing that you lose yourself completely in the activity. You feel thrilled just to be doing whatever it is you are doing, whether it's running a race, writing a story, painting a picture, or simply gazing at a sunset.

this feeling by honing your ability to concentrate intently. In time, you may learn to find joy in almost anything. All you have to do is immerse yourself completely in the experience.

Thich Nhat Hanh is a Buddhist monk from Vietnam and a noted peace advocate. In his book *Peace Is Every Step,* he describes the pleasure of doing something most people probably don't consider fun: washing dishes. He also explains why learning to appreciate even the ordinary things in life is important:

I enjoy taking my time with each dish, being fully aware of the dish, the water, and each movement of my hands... If I am incapable of washing dishes joyfully, if I want to finish them quickly so I can go and have dessert, I will be equally incapable of enjoying my dessert. With the fork in my hand, I will be thinking about what to do next, and the texture and flavor of the dessert, together with the pleasure of eating it, will be lost.

Meditation helps you develop this ability to live life to the utmost. For many people, that may be the best reason of all to meditate. In the following chapters, you'll read more about what meditation is and how to do it. You'll also learn more about why meditation is such a valuable skill to know.

Two

The Relaxation Response

Hans Selye is one of the most important figures in the history of stress research. As a young scientist, though, he made his share of blunders. In the 1930s, Selye wanted to test the effects of a particular substance in rats, so he decided to give them a shot of the substance every day. The only problem was his clumsiness. When Selye tried to inject the rats, he often would miss the mark, drop the rats, and spend half the day chasing them around the lab.

After months of this, Selye was finally ready to examine the rats. He found that they had developed three physical changes. First, the rats' adrenal glands, small glands located just above each of the two kidneys, were enlarged. Second, their immune tissues, part of the body's infection-fighting system, had shrunk. Third, the rats had peptic ulcers, sores in the lining of the stomach or upper small intestine.

At first, Selye was elated. He believed that he had discovered the effects of the substance he was testing. His high hopes were soon dashed, however. Selye had injected a second group of rats with nothing more than saltwater. These rats also went through several months of fumbling, dropping, and chasing. And they, too, developed the same three physical changes. Rather than give up on the experiment, though, Selye tried to figure out what the two groups of rats had in common. He soon realized that it must be his clumsy way of giving a shot, which was creating a lot of stress for the animals.

Selye had discovered a crucial fact: Stress can make you sick. Another scientist named Walter Cannon had found the reason for this fact a few decades before. In the early 1900s, Cannon first described the fight-or-flight response, the body's automatic reaction to any threat—real or imagined, physical or emotional. It is this response that gives stress its power to help or harm.

Fight or Flight
Imagine that you are hunting for your dinner in the wild,

The Meditation Prescription

If stress can make you sick, then using meditation to manage stress should help keep you well. Scientific studies have shown that meditation can, in fact, help prevent or reduce the symptoms of several diseases.

- *In one study of people with high blood pressure, meditation lowered blood pressure about as much as medication did.*
- *In one study of people with blood vessel disease, meditation decreased the hardening of the arteries that may lead to a heart attack or stroke.*
- *In one study of people with cancer, meditation reduced emotional distress and several physical symptoms, including tiredness.*
- *In one study of people with fibromyalgia—a condition that causes pain, tiredness, and sleep problems— meditation decreased the symptoms.*
- *In one study of people with a wide range of long-term illnesses, meditation led to less emotional distress and fewer physical symptoms, such as pain.*

armed only with a club. Suddenly, a snarling beast charges toward you. If you thought you could overpower the animal, you might stand and fight. If you thought the animal was stronger, you might, instead, turn and run as fast as you could.

The fight-or-flight response readies your body for either reaction. This response is rooted in the part of your brain called the hypothalamus. When faced with a threat, the hypothalamus sets off a chain of events that causes the release of certain hormones. Hormones are chemicals that are produced in one part of the body, then carried through the bloodstream to other parts, where they have specific effects. As stress hormones travel throughout your body, several effects occur.

- Your body draws on its energy stores. Sugar and fat pour into your bloodstream. These fuels give you a quick burst of energy.

- Your breathing becomes faster. This supplies your body with more oxygen, which helps it use the fuel for energy production.

- Your heart beats faster, and your blood pressure increases. These changes help bring more blood to places where you need it, such as to your muscles and your brain. The blood carries fuel and oxygen to these areas.

- Your muscles tense up. This lets you brace for a fight or prepare to run. You may even feel your jaw tighten or your fists clench.

- Your digestion slows down, as does your infection-fighting system. This energy is more urgently needed elsewhere in an emergency.

These changes might be handy if you were faced, for example, with a hungry tiger. Most stressful situations in modern life, however, don't require much wrestling or running. Your body, unfortunately, can't tell the difference between the threat of a wild animal and the threat of a hard math test. It goes into exactly the same state of high alert.

Once you fight off or escape from an attacking animal, the threat is over. Many sources of stress in modern life don't end so quickly, however. Maybe you're stressed out

Most stressful situations in modern life don't require much wrestling or running. Your body, unfortunately, can't tell the difference. It goes into exactly the same state of high alert.

because your math teacher is demanding, your parents are always fighting, or gangs have taken over your neighborhood. These kinds of situations can drag on for a long time. Such long-term stress can wear away at your body and your mind. Eventually, long-term stress can play a role in causing a host of physical and emotional health problems, including high blood pressure, heart disease, muscle aches and pains, digestive problems, frequent infections, anxiety, and depression.

How Stressed Out Are You?

Make a copy of these two pages, and check "yes" or "no" for each question below.

Yes	No	Question
		1. Do you often have negative thoughts or feelings about yourself?
		2. Do you feel uncomfortable with recent changes in your body?
		3. Do you have trouble making or keeping friends?
		4. Do you live in an unsafe home or neighborhood?
		5. Do you have trouble getting along with your parents?
		6. Does someone in your family have a serious illness or problem?
		7. Has your family gone through financial difficulties lately?
		8. Have you recently changed schools or moved to a new home?

Yes	No	Question
		9. Do you feel frustrated or overwhelmed by the demands at school?
		10. Do you have trouble finding enough time for all your activities?
		11. Do you feel as if you have to meet unrealistically high standards?
		12. Do you often feel that stress is getting the best of you?
		13. Have you had a serious accident or illness within the last year?
		14. Have your parents separated or divorced within the last year?
		15. Has someone close to you died within the last year?

Scoring

For questions 1–12, give yourself 5 points for each "yes" answer. For questions 13–15, give yourself 15 points for each "yes" answer. Then add up your points.

15 or more points: You have significant sources of stress in your life right now. Meditation might

Kaneland High School Library
47 W 326 Keslinger Road
Maple Park, IL 60151

How Stressed Out Are You? (Continued)

help you manage the stress. If you often feel scared, worried, sad, or angry, you should also discuss your feelings with a parent, counselor, or other trusted adult.

5–10 points: You are under a fair amount of stress. Meditation might help you keep stress from getting out of hand. Remember, though, that people react to the same situation differently. Understand your feelings, and seek help if you have any trouble handling them.

0 points: Congratulations! You seem to have a relatively low-stress life. Low stress doesn't mean no stress, however. You can still benefit from meditation. Also, learning to meditate now will give you the tools you can use later if new sources of stress should arise.

Rest and Relaxation

If left unchecked, the effects of stress could cause a lot of damage. Luckily, the body also has a built-in way of undoing these changes, which is called the relaxation response. This is a state of deep rest that reverses the physical and emotional effects of the fight-or-flight response. While the effects of stress occur involuntarily, you can learn to call up the relaxation response at will by practicing meditation.

Stress has been the subject of scientific study for a century. It wasn't until the late 1960s, however, that scientists first began to look at the relaxation response. At the time, a doctor named Herbert Benson was studying blood pressure in monkeys. He was approached by several people who practiced Transcendental Meditation (TM). TM is a form of meditation in which people focus on a mantra—a special word or sound that is repeated over and over. These people claimed that they could lower their blood pressure using meditation. Benson was uninterested at first, since their claim went against the accepted medical wisdom of the day. However, the TM adherents refused to go away. Finally, Benson agreed to measure their physical responses.

Surprisingly, Benson found that meditating did indeed decrease their metabolism (the group of basic physical processes that keep the body running.) It also reduced their breathing rate and heart rate. In addition, meditation led to a distinct pattern of brain waves, the rhythmic ups and downs seen in the electric currents within the brain. During meditation, the people had more of the kind of brain waves typically seen during rest, and fewer of the kind typically seen during waking activity. Benson named this set of effects the relaxation response.

Ironically, one thing meditation *didn't* do among these subjects was lower their blood pressure. However, they already had low blood pressure to begin with, which may be why it didn't drop much in Benson's study. Later research has shown that, in fact, meditation sometimes can reduce blood pressure that is too high. A decrease in blood pressure is another part of the relaxation response.

Today, one of the main reasons people of all ages meditate is to relax and manage stress. If meditation once was considered a little strange, it now has gone mainstream. Harvard Medical School, where Benson conducted his work, offers courses that teach doctors about the health benefits of meditation. The National Institutes of Health sponsor research on the subject. And the Junior Girl Scouts offer a Stress Less badge. One activity for earning the badge is to learn a breathing exercise that can be used to call up the relaxation response.

The Beatles and the Maharishi

The Beatles didn't just revolutionize rock and roll. They also helped introduce the Western world to meditation. In the 1960s, the Beatles became followers of Maharishi Mahesh Yogi. The Maharishi had developed TM, his own brand of meditation based on ancient Hindu practices. He attracted other famous fans, too, including actors Shirley MacLaine and Mia Farrow. For a few years, the Maharishi was seen as a leader by the "flower children," a group of young hippies who preached love and peace. Soon, though, other forms of meditation began to rival TM in popularity. The Maharishi started to fade from public view. Nevertheless, he deserves much of the credit for making meditation a household word in the United States.

How to Experience Less Stress

Many forms of meditation can be used to bring on relaxation. All they have to do is meet two requirements. First, you need to pick something to focus on. This can be a repeated word, phrase, sound, or activity. It can even be your own breathing. Second, you need to passively disregard other thoughts that may come to mind. This doesn't mean trying to force yourself to focus, however. Instead, it means gently guiding your mind back whenever it starts to wander.

Below are some basic guidelines for applying these ideas. Like any new skill, calling up the relaxation response can take some practice. With a little time and effort, however, almost anyone can learn to do it by following these steps.

1. Pick a focus word, phrase, sound, or activity. Some people choose a word or phrase that has meaning for them, such as "Hail Mary," "shalom," or "peace." Others prefer a sound, such as "om." Still others prefer a rhythmic activity, such as breathing, walking on a footpath, or pedaling a stationary bicycle. (Of course, you would need to pay attention to your surroundings if you were walking or cycling in traffic.)

2. Sit in a comfortable position. You also can lie down, but remember that the goal is to meditate, not sleep. Close your eyes, if you wish. Try to relax all your muscles in turn, moving from your feet to your head. If you have a lot of trouble sitting quietly, a rhythmic activity that lets you move around is another option.

3. Breathe slowly and naturally. As you do so, start to repeat your focus word, phrase, or sound on each breath out. You can do this silently or aloud. If you have chosen to focus on an activity, do it in time with your breathing as well. For example, you might take four steps on every breath in and four more steps on every breath out.

4. Passively disregard other thoughts that may arise. Don't worry if you become distracted at times. This is normal. Just let other thoughts, feelings, and sensations pass right through your mind. Then gently return your mind to the focus point.

5. Practice every day, if you can. Start out meditating for ten minutes or less at a time. As it becomes easier, you may work up to twenty minutes. Don't get too wrapped up in meeting a time goal, however. The wonderful thing about meditation is that you can simply accept it as it comes. There is no such thing as a failing grade in meditation.

Look at step 3 above. You'll see that breathing is an important part of meditating for relaxation. Remember that meditation involves focusing your mind on a particular thing or activity. If you want to use meditation to relax, the focus point should be something that is repeated in a steady rhythm. If you've ever played a musical instrument, you may have used a metronome. This is a device that helps you mark time by making a regularly repeated ticking sound. Breathing is like a natural metronome within your body. It helps you set and keep a regular rhythm.

Three

The Mind/Body/Spirit Link

Carlos always had trouble in math class. Whenever the teacher started talking, his mind would wander. Then Carlos began to meditate every night at home. He found that his ability to concentrate in class improved, and his math grades soon did, too.

Mai loved gymnastics. She practiced every day after school. In practices, she could do difficult turns and leaps on the balance beam over and over without falling off. In meets, however, she lost her balance every time. Then Mai began to meditate. She found that it improved her ability to focus, which helped her do her best in meets.

What's In It for You?

Different things are important to different people. What matters most to you? The following test can help you figure it out. This information, in turn, can help you decide which approach to meditation suits you best. On another sheet of paper, rate your answer to each question from 1 for "not very much" to 5 for "a lot."

Rating	Question
Less *More* 1 2 3 4 5	1. Do you want to improve your performance in school?
1 2 3 4 5	2. Do you ever have trouble paying attention in class?
1 2 3 4 5	3. Do you stress out and forget everything you know at test time?
1 2 3 4 5	4. Do you like to get totally wrapped up in drawing or writing?
1 2 3 4 5	5. Do you enjoy activities that challenge you mentally?
1 2 3 4 5	6. Do you want to improve your performance in a sport?
1 2 3 4 5	7. Do you ever "choke" when you're playing in a big game?
1 2 3 4 5	8. Do you have an interest in yoga, t'ai chi, or martial arts?

Rating	Question
Less *More* 1 2 3 4 5	9. Do you like to unwind by walking, running, or cycling?
1 2 3 4 5	10. Do you enjoy activities that challenge you physically?
1 2 3 4 5	11. Do you want to improve your ability to connect with others?
1 2 3 4 5	12. Do you ever think about your place in the larger universe?
1 2 3 4 5	13. Do you have an interest in religion or spiritual matters?
1 2 3 4 5	14. Do you ever wonder about the meaning of life and love?
1 2 3 4 5	15. Do you enjoy activities that help you grow spiritually?

Scoring

Add up the numbers for questions 1–5. Is the total number 10 or greater? You may be interested in learning more about how meditation can help you mentally. See the section of this chapter titled "Mind: Meditation for School."

Add up the numbers for questions 6–10. Is the total number 10 or greater? You may be interested in learning more about how meditation can help you physically. See the section of this chapter titled "Body: Meditation for Sports."

What's In It for You?
(Continued)

Add up the numbers for questions 11–15. Is the total number 10 or greater? You may be interested in learning more about how meditation can help you spiritually. See the section of this chapter titled "Spirit: Meditation for Self-Discovery."

You may find that you scored 10 or higher in more than one area. Maybe you're most interested in improving at a sport, for example, but you also would like to raise your grades and feel more connected to others. That's great! Meditation can help you grow in all these directions at once.

You've given some thought to your priorities. Now it may help to turn what you've learned into statements about what you want to get out of meditation. Complete the sentences below, writing your answers on a separate sheet of paper. Of course, you can easily change your statements later, as your desires, needs, and abilities change. Meditation is very adaptable.

The main thing I want to get out of meditation right now is

_____.

Other things I would like to get out of meditation now are

_____.

One thing I hope to gain from meditation in the future is

_____.

Jon's parents were divorced last year. He had recently moved with his mom to a new town, where he didn't know anyone. Sometimes Jon felt lost and confused, as if his whole world had been turned upside down. Then Jon began to meditate. It helped him feel more at peace with himself and his feelings. This, in turn, made it easier for him to connect with other people and make new friends.

Meditation can affect you on every level: mind, body, and spirit. You may get one thing out of meditation; the student sitting next to you may get another. It all depends on who you are and what you need at that moment. This is one of the truly special things about meditation.

Meditation can affect you on every level: mind, body, and spirit. It all depends on who you are and what you need at that moment.

Yoga and Zen

The three-part focus on mind, body, and spirit dates back to the beginnings of meditation. Hinduism, the major religion of India, has one of the oldest traditions of meditation in the world. Mantras play a big role in the spiritual side of that tradition. Hindus believe that these sacred sounds were gifts from the divine spirit to ancient seers. For example, the mantra "om" is thought to be the sound of the vibration of the universe. Today, mantras are still passed down from spiritual teachers to their students.

However, Hinduism also includes yoga, a system of special exercises that develop the body and mind. Many Americans think of yoga as a form of physical exercise that uses special postures to stretch, strengthen, and align the body. Yoga-based exercise classes are taught at health clubs and community centers all over the country. Traditionally, though, yoga is more than just a physical workout. It also is a system of mental discipline that involves meditation. Yoga meditation often makes use of special postures and breathing exercises.

Buddhism, another of the world's major religions, was founded in India by a spiritual teacher—Buddha—who preached the importance of mindfulness. This is the practice of focusing your attention on whatever you are experiencing from moment to moment. For example, you might focus intently on the look, taste, smell, and feel of a piece of fruit you're eating. Buddha taught that there were four foundations of mindfulness: awareness of the body, awareness of feelings, awareness of thoughts and mental states, and awareness of the laws of experience that tie things together. If you think for a minute about these types of awareness, you'll see that they include being aware of your mind, body, and spirit.

Buddhism eventually spread across Asia and sprouted several branches. One branch, called Zen, puts particular stress on the use of meditation to develop mindfulness. The goal of Zen is to attain spiritual enlightenment. Meditation is thought to be the key to doing this. Today, the religion of Zen Buddhism is practiced mainly in Japan. However, there also is a growing interest in Zen ideas in the United States. It's not uncommon to hear people talk about "mindful eating" or the "Zen of basketball." By this, they mean being completely focused on the moment-to-moment experience, whether it involves eating an orange or playing in a basketball game.

It's not uncommon to hear people talk about "mindful eating" or the "Zen of basketball." By this, they mean being completely focused on the moment-to-moment experience, whether it involves eating an orange or playing in a basketball game.

What do Hindu yoga and Zen mindfulness have in common? Both stress that meditation affects not only the spirit but also the body and mind. In addition, both have given rise to forms of meditation that everyone can use. You don't have to practice these religions (or any religion at all) to get the physical and mental benefits of meditation. The benefits are open to anyone with any beliefs.

Christian and Jewish Meditation

Christians and Jews have adapted various forms of meditation for their beliefs. For example, some use "Our Father," "Hail Mary," or "shalom" as focus words. In addition, meditation is closely related to the Christian and Jewish practice of contemplative prayer. This is different from praying to ask for help. It involves praying in order to draw closer to God or reflect on spiritual truths. Some people regard this as a form of meditation in which the focus is on God.

Mind: Meditation for School

One way to use the mental power of meditation is for school. Have you ever sat through a class or read a chapter in your textbook only to find that you didn't remember a thing about it afterward? Your body was going through the motions, but your mind was elsewhere. Meditation teaches you to recognize when your mind is wandering off so that you can bring it back. This is how concentration grows. Meditation also helps you learn to let go of all those distracting thoughts and daydreams.

Meditation helps you manage stress, as well. Too much stress makes it hard to do your best on tests. As a result, stressed-out students often see their grades fall. Their attitude toward school and themselves may suffer, too. In addition, some students react to stress by getting into trouble at school and at home.

Does learning to meditate really help students do better in school? Scientific studies suggest that it may. One study, for example, included 362 students from three schools in Taiwan. First, the students took several tests of mental ability. Then, some were randomly chosen to take part in a meditation program, while others were not. The program lasted six months to a year. Afterward, all the students were tested again. The researchers found that those who had meditated showed greater gains in their scores on tests of intelligence, creativity, and other mental abilities.

Several schools around the United States are starting to take note. They use meditation to help students stay focused and to manage stress. Jennifer Johnston helps direct one such program at the Mind/Body Medical Institute in Boston. Johnston's job involves traveling to schools around the country teaching students and teachers how to relax and better manage their stress. She shows them how to meditate by focusing on their breathing. She also teaches them yoga moves and other simple meditation methods. "Often, students don't even know how stressed out they're feeling until they give themselves a few moments to stop feeling it," says Johnston. Research on this program has shown that students who take part in meditation often go on to have a higher grade point average, increased self-esteem, better work habits, and fewer absences.

If your school doesn't offer a program such as this, you can create one for yourself. All you have to do is set aside a few minutes each day for meditation. Many students find that meditating for ten minutes in the morning before leaving for school sets a calm tone for the day. If you're the type who is always running for the school bus, however,

Mini-Meditation for Taking Tests

You start to take an important test, when suddenly your mind goes blank. You knew the material last night. Why can't you remember it now? All you can think about is your pounding heart, dry mouth, and sweaty palms. For many people, taking tests is very stressful. If you find yourself in this situation, you probably won't have time for a full meditation session. However, a quick mini-meditation may help you calm your mind and relax your body, allowing you to do your best on the test.

1. *Breathe slowly and deeply. Begin silently counting backward from ten to zero, saying one number to yourself for each breath out.*

2. *Ask yourself how you feel when you get to zero. If you are still feeling stressed out, start slowly counting back up to ten.*

you may want to wait until later in the day to practice meditation. For example, you might meditate when you first get home in the afternoon or right before you start your homework in the evening.

Body: Meditation for Sports

Tiger Woods is one of the best golfers of all time. In 1997, he won his first Masters Tournament, becoming the youngest golfer (at age twenty-one) and the first African American to win this major title. Woods is known not only for his skill but also for his composure and intense focus during tournaments. He learned to meditate as a child from his mother, who has a Buddhist background. Woods has said that he now meditates daily without even thinking about it, because it is second nature to him. Many people think that this has played an important role in his success.

Meditation helps us access our physical power, which is useful in sports. Top athletes often say that focus is the key to peak performance. Of course, practicing regularly and staying in shape are important. But to perform their best, athletes often try to get into a state of complete focus called flow. Meditation can improve the ability of a person to bring on that state at will.

You can use the ability to concentrate in any sport. The idea is the same whether you are trying to keep your eye on

To perform their best, athletes often try to get into a state of complete focus called flow. Meditation can improve the ability of a person to bring on that state at will.

the ball in baseball, shoot a basket in basketball, or land a jump in figure skating. Many athletes who meditate daily like to add an extra meditation session right before an important game or contest.

To see how focus can help your sports performance, try a simple exercise: First, dribble a basketball without paying much attention to what you are doing. Have someone else count how many times you can bounce the ball before you lose control of it. Then, dribble the basketball again, but this time intently focus on the ball. If your mind wanders from the ball, bring it back. Try to imagine that the ball is tied to your hand with an elastic band. Each time you push the ball down, the elastic band pulls it back up to your hand. Once more, have the other person count how many times you bounce the ball. Chances are that you'll see a big improvement.

There also are some sports where the activity itself can be a form of moving meditation. Long-distance running is an example. Runners often say they lose themselves in the rhythmic rise and fall of their own steps. It's easy to see how this is similar to focusing on your rising and falling breath.

Yoga and t'ai chi are two popular activities with especially close ties to meditation. As described previously, yoga grew out of Hindu practices in India. T'ai chi, which began as a martial art in China more than one thousand years ago, is a system of physical exercise that uses slow, flowing movements. Like yoga, however, t'ai chi is more than just a method of physical exercise; it also uses special breathing and meditation techniques, which are thought to promote overall health.

Spirit: Meditation for Self-Discovery

One way to use the spiritual power of meditation is for self-discovery. As you've learned, meditation is really the act of observing your own thoughts, feelings, and sensations. You can use this process to learn more about yourself. Afterward, you may find yourself wanting to ponder some Big Questions, such as "Who am I?" and "What does it all mean?"

The link between meditation and deep thinking can be seen in the history of the word itself. Sanskrit is the classical

Meditation is really the act of observing your own thoughts, feelings, and sensations. You may find yourself wanting to ponder some Big Questions, such as "Who am I?" and "What does it all mean?"

As Easy as Breathing

Yoga can be practiced as a physical workout or as a mental discipline. In either case, special breathing methods play an important role. The following are some yoga breathing exercises that you can use to relax when getting ready to meditate. You can also use the exercises as mini-meditations in themselves. To do this, simply focus on your own breathing.

Belly Breathing

1. Lie on your back in a comfortable position. (You can also do this exercise seated or standing.) Put one hand on your belly, just below your navel.
2. Breathe in slowly. Try to breathe deep into your abdomen, not high into your chest. Your hand should rise slightly with your belly.
3. Breathe out slowly. Your hand should fall as your belly flattens.
4. Repeat several times. Keep focusing on your breathing.

Notice how your hand continues to rise and fall in a slow, even manner.

Side-to-Side Breathing

1. Sit in a comfortable position. Lift your right hand to your nose. Fold your pointer and middle fingers over into your palm. This leaves your thumb free on one side, and your ring and pinkie fingers free on the other side.
2. Press your thumb against the right side of your nose, closing off your right nostril. Breathe out slowly through your left nostril.
3. Breathe in slowly through your left nostril. Release your thumb.
4. Press your ring and pinkie fingers against the left side of your nose, closing off your left nostril. Breathe out slowly through your right nostril.
5. Breathe in slowly through your right nostril. Release your ring and pinkie fingers.
6. Repeat steps 2–5 several times.

As Easy as Breathing (Continued)

Spine-Tingling Breathing

1. Sit in a comfortable position. Close your eyes. Bring the focus of your attention to the base of your spine.
2. Breathe in slowly. As you do, draw your awareness gradually up your spine. Your focus should travel up your back, through your neck, and to your skull.
3. Breathe out slowly. As you do, bring your awareness gradually back down to the base of your spine.
4. Repeat several times.

Hot and Cold Breathing

1. Sit in a comfortable position. Close your eyes.
2. Breathe in slowly through your nose. Notice how cool the air feels coming in.
3. Breathe out slowly through your mouth. Notice how much warmer the air feels going out.
4. Repeat several times.

language of India and Hinduism. The word *meditation* comes from the Sanskrit *medha,* which can be translated as "doing the wisdom." In other words, meditation can help make you wiser. The word also traces back to the Latin *meditari,* which means "to ponder." In other words, meditation can help you think deeply about whatever is on your mind.

Since meditation often gives rise to deep thoughts, it's no wonder that many people use meditation for personal growth. First, they meditate to become calm and relaxed. Then, while they are still deeply relaxed, they engage in contemplation. This is the act of reflecting on a certain experience, issue, or spiritual truth in an effort to gain greater insight.

Contemplation is at the heart of religious meditation. People of all faiths use contemplation to ponder the nature of God and the mystery of creation. However, contemplation can also be used to reflect on nonreligious matters. If you have a problem in your life, calm reflection may help you think of a solution. If you are trying to make a difficult choice, it may help you sort out your options. If you are trying to achieve a goal, calm reflection may help you stay focused on what you need to do.

Contemplating Lovingkindness

To see how contemplation can be used for personal growth, try this exercise: Think about the way a loving mother feels toward her baby. She gives her love freely and without any conditions, and she doesn't expect anything in return. This is a quality that Buddhists call "lovingkindness." Psychologists often call it "unconditional love." Whatever term you use, this is a way of caring about yourself and others that can be strengthened through meditation and contemplation. Follow the steps below to explore your own capacity for lovingkindness.

1. Sit or lie in a comfortable position. Close your eyes. Take several slow, deep breaths to relax. As you move through the following steps, try not to rush. If you start to feel impatient or annoyed, don't worry. Just gently return your mind to whatever you are contemplating.

2. Allow your heart to fill with lovingkindness. First, direct this love and caring toward yourself. Think of something kind or good that you have done. Notice the happiness that comes from remembering this act. Now think of some ability or trait that you like in yourself. Once again, notice the pleasure that comes from reflecting on your strength.

3. Imagine the face of someone you consider a close friend. As you hold that image in your mind, direct the flow of love toward the person. Think of something kind or generous that the person has done. Notice the gratitude or respect that comes from remembering.

4. Imagine the face of someone you see regularly but don't know well. As you hold that image in your mind, direct the flow of love toward the person. Think of something about the person that you like or admire. Notice the positive feelings that come from remembering.

As you've seen, the mind, body, and spirit are all connected. Meditation is a way to tie these elements together. It can be used to focus the mind, relax the body, explore the spirit—or accomplish all three. The wonderful thing is that it can be geared to your individual personality and needs. Meditation can be as large or as small a part of your life as you want it to be.

Four

Minding Your
Mindfulness

How much attention do you pay to your surroundings? Chances are that you think you are at least fairly attentive. After all, you manage to juggle the demands of several classes. You keep up a social life with friends and family members. You even find time for chores at home and a hobby or two. There is a difference, however, between simply living your life and living it mindfully. The latter involves fully focusing your attention on whatever you are experiencing from moment to moment.

To see what this is like, try being mindful of the sounds around you. First, take several slow, deep breaths to relax.

Close your eyes, if you wish. Then, direct your full attention to the sounds in your environment. Don't strain to hear them. Just take them as they come. Try not to analyze the sounds, either. Just hear them as pure sounds, without trying to read any meaning into them. For example, if a phone rings, notice the tone, but don't try to guess who is on the other end. Listen to the silences between sounds as well. If your mind wanders, gently guide it back.

Did you notice some sounds that you were unaware of earlier? If so, you now know what it feels like to listen more mindfully. The benefits of greater mindfulness are many. Your senses seem sharper. You become more attuned to your thoughts and feelings. In short, your self-awareness is raised.

You can develop greater mindfulness through meditation. First, use deep breathing to become calm and relaxed. Then, focus your attention on some aspect of your experience. Your focus point can be anything. It can be a certain sensation—whatever you can see, hear, smell, taste, or touch. It can be the feeling of your own muscles in action. It can be your thoughts or emotions at this particular time. Or it can be all of the above as they relate to one activity. For example, you might notice your sensations, actions, thoughts, and emotions as you walk the dog or eat breakfast or make your bed. Anything you can do can be done mindfully.

A Mind Full of Mindfulness

How mindful are you of your surroundings? Ask yourself these questions:

- *Can you find a certain outfit in your closet by touch alone?*
- *Can you pick out the sounds of different instruments in a band?*
- *Can you tell what is cooking for dinner using only smell?*
- *Can you pick out the flavors of different ingredients in a food?*
- *Can you describe exactly how your body reacts to stress?*

A Taste of Mindfulness

To get another taste of mindfulness, try mindful eating: Have an apple (or another fruit you like) on hand. First, relax with some slow, deep breaths. Then, focus on what is happening here and now, and let go of other thoughts. Bring your focus to the apple. Take a few minutes to turn it around in your hands. Notice its color, shape, and texture. Next, bring the apple to your nose, and notice its smell. Now, take a bite. Chew slowly, and let your tongue soak up the flavor. Enjoy the taste as if you had never eaten an apple before. Let yourself savor the experience of eating.

The concept of mindfulness may have its roots in Buddhism, but it has been adapted to modern health care,

Scanning Your Body

A body scan is a form of mindfulness meditation. It involves focusing attention on your body, section by section. All the while, you're noticing and accepting how you feel at the moment. It can be a particularly powerful tool for people who are uncomfortable with their bodies for one reason or another. This is common among teenagers, who may not yet be at ease with their rapidly changing bodies.

A body scan also can be very helpful for people who tense up their muscles when they are feeling stressed. In addition, it can help those who have an illness or injury that causes pain. The body scan won't fix the physical problem, of course. It can, however, relieve the psychological distress that often makes the pain feel worse. Below are the basic steps to follow when doing a body scan.

1. Lie in a comfortable position. Close your eyes. Take several slow, deep breaths to relax.
2. Focus your attention on the toes of your left foot. Let yourself feel any and all sensations there. If you feel any discomfort or itchiness, accept it. If you don't feel anything, that's fine, too. Then, imagine directing your

breathing to your left toes. Try to feel what it would be like if you were breathing in through your toes and breathing out from them.

3. Move on to the next part of your body when you're ready. Try to leave behind any sensations you felt as you move from region to region. Gradually move through your body in this order: left toes, left foot, left calf, left thigh, right toes, right foot, right calf, right thigh, abdomen, buttocks, chest, back, left fingers, left hand, left lower arm, left upper arm, right fingers, right hand, right lower arm, right upper arm, neck, head.

4. Don't rush the process. When you come to the end, finish with some deep, slow breaths. Give yourself a few minutes to enjoy the relaxation before you stand up.

Do you have trouble imagining yourself breathing into and out of various parts of your body, as described in step 2 above? If this is hard for you, imagine instead that each part of your body, in turn, is floating on warm water or a cloud. Or, imagine that each part of your body is filled with a glowing white light or your favorite color. Personalize your body scan to make it work for you.

as well. Several researchers have looked at the physical and emotional benefits of mindfulness. One of the leaders in this area is Jon Kabat-Zinn at the University of Massachusetts Medical School.

In one study, Kabat-Zinn and his co-workers found that training in mindfulness meditation helped people with long-term pain to reduce their discomfort. In a second study, they found that such training helped people decrease the symptoms of anxiety disorders (conditions in which long-lasting or intense feelings of fear, worry, or nervousness occur for no reason). In a third study, Kabat-Zinn and his co-workers showed that adding mindfulness meditation to standard medical treatment sped up the healing of a skin condition known as psoriasis.

Mindfulness is also at the core of some offshoots of Buddhist meditation that are currently popular in the United States. One of these is insight meditation, also known as Vipassana meditation. It is derived from a form of Buddhism practiced in Southeast Asia. However, as with other types of meditation, it often is used for nonreligious purposes, as well.

Imagine Yourself Relaxed

Tibetan Buddhist meditation is another kind of meditation that has been adapted to American life. In addition to mindfulness, such meditation often uses imagery. This involves focusing your mind on imagined sights, sounds, smells, tastes, or other sensations. It is similar to mindfulness, except that the focus is on imagined rather than real experiences. In Tibetan Buddhism, the goal is to call up spiritual forces. Imagery, however, can also be used simply to deepen relaxation.

To combine imagery with meditation, take several long, deep breaths to relax. Then, imagine a particular experience or scene. Try to make the experience as realistic as possible. For example, let's say you imagine lying in a grassy field on a sunny day. In your mind's eye, you might notice vivid shades of green and blue. You might also notice the smell of the grass and the warmth of the sun on your skin. The more senses you can bring into the picture, the better.

Some people use imagery meditation as a tool to improve performance. Let's say you have a piano recital coming up. You're having trouble with one particular part of your piece. The harder you try to force your fingers to play it, the more tense they get, and the worse you perform. You might try using imagery meditation for ten minutes or so before each practice session. First, focus on your breathing to get into a state of deep relaxation. Then, imagine yourself playing that section with ease. In your imagination, feel the muscles in your hands as they move your fingers. Notice the smoothness of the piano keys as you touch them. Notice the sound made by each.

Mentally going over a task this way can help you learn it. Of course, it doesn't take the place of actual practice. However, it may give you the calmness and confidence you need to make the most of your practice time. Many world-class musicians use this method to prepare for performances. Top athletes use it before competitions. And you can use it to enhance just about any skill.

Smile Power

Find a picture of a classic statue of Buddha. You'll notice that he wears a slight smile that stands for peace and joy. You, too, can share this happy feeling. Here is a quick exercise in mindful smiling.

1. *Take several slow, deep breaths to relax. Then, form your lips into a peaceful smile. First, notice how the rest of your face changes. Next, notice how the rest of your body responds. Finally, notice how your mind responds. Does your mood lighten a bit, too?*

2. *Keep smiling for several minutes. Go about your ordinary activities, but pay attention to how you act and how others react. Do you notice any differences in your behavior? Do other people smile back at you?*

3. *Smile even when others can't see. You don't have to save this exercise for public places. You also can use it while sitting alone or talking on the phone. Does smiling make you feel more at peace even then?*

Mentally going over a task can help you learn it. Many world-class musicians use this method to prepare for performances. Top athletes use it before competitions.

Questions and Answers

All right, you're convinced. You want to try meditation. It may take some trial and error, but just about everybody can find a form of meditation that works for them, including you. To make your search easier, here are the answers to some common questions that beginners often ask.

Question: What if I get sleepy during meditation?

Answer: This is a very common problem. First, ask yourself if you're getting enough sleep. Most young people need eight to ten hours of sleep each night in order to feel rested and refreshed the next day. If you're out like a light as soon as your head hits the pillow, you may not be getting all the sleep you need.

Even people who get plenty of sleep sometimes feel drowsy during meditation, however. This is often a sign that your mind is rebelling. Feeling foggy is one way for your mind to resist the quietly alert state of meditation. You may need to give your mind a gentle wake-up nudge. If you're lying down, try sitting up straight. If your eyes are closed, try opening them. If this doesn't work, you may want to start meditating while you walk, practice yoga, or do t'ai chi.

Question: What if I feel restless or bored?

Answer: Don't worry. Many people feel this way when they first start meditating. Instead of fighting such feelings, just take note of them as you would anything else. Then gently guide your mind back to the focus point. Like sleepiness, boredom or restlessness can be a sign that your rebellious mind doesn't want to settle down. With time, however, the feelings should fade as you learn to enjoy meditation. If they don't, try other forms of meditation until you find one you like.

Question: Do I have to sit in a special position?

Answer: No. Many pictures of people meditating show them sitting in the lotus pose (shown on opposite page). This involves sitting cross-legged on the floor with a straight back. In the full lotus position, you put your right foot on top of your left thigh and your left foot on top your right thigh. Many people find it difficult or im-possible to sit this way, though. An alternative is the half lotus (shown on p. 64), in which you put one foot on top of its opposite thigh, and leave the other foot on the floor underneath its opposite thigh. If you try the half lotus, be sure both knees touch the floor, so that you aren't tilted too much to one side. Also, try switching the foot that is

Full Lotus

Half Lotus

on top from day to day, so that you don't put all the strain on one leg.

The most important thing, however, is that you find a sitting position that is comfortable for you. This can mean a full lotus, a half lotus, or no lotus at all. Some people meditate sitting in a chair. Other types of meditation can be done lying down, standing, or even walking.

Question: Can I keep my eyes open?

Answer: Yes, if you wish. Many people like to close their eyes while meditating. This helps them focus on their inner experience without being distracted by the outside world. However, some people find that shutting their eyes leads to drowsiness or makes them nervous. One alternative is keeping your eyes wide open. Unfortunately, this makes it much harder to tune out distractions. A better alternative may be keeping your eyes only half open, gazing downward at the floor.

Question: What should I do with my hands?

Answer: Whatever feels comfortable for you. You may have seen people meditating with their hands resting palms up on their knees. The thumb and pointer finger on each hand are brought together to form a small circle. This is a traditional hand position, but you don't have to use it. You can also simply place your hands on your thighs or fold them in your lap, if that feels more natural.

Question: When and where should I meditate?

Answer: That depends on you. Many people like to meditate first thing in the morning. They say that it sets a relaxed tone for the whole day. Others find it more convenient to meditate in the afternoon or evening. Whatever time you pick, it helps if you can meditate at least once a day. Like anything else, meditation gets easier and becomes more effective with regular practice.

The ideal spot to meditate is a quiet place where you won't be disturbed by other people. You don't have to find a lonely mountaintop, however. Some students meditate in the classroom during a few minutes of silence. Others meditate in their bedroom when they first wake up or right before they fall asleep. Still others prefer to

Like anything else, meditation gets easier and becomes more effective with regular practice.

meditate outdoors in their backyard or in a park near their home. The key is simply to find a place that feels safe and doesn't have too many distractions.

Question: Do I need to wear special clothing?

Answer: Not really. You can do some types of meditation wherever you happen to be, wearing whatever clothes you have on. However, it always helps to get comfortable, especially if you plan to meditate for several minutes.

Loose clothes or workout gear are a good choice for longer meditation sessions (skin-tight jeans can make it nearly impossible to sit in a cross-legged position, if that's what you want to do). Because body temperature tends to drop as you relax, you may also want to have a light sweater or jacket on hand in case you get chilly.

Question: Do I need to take a meditation class?

Answer: Not necessarily. Many people teach themselves to meditate with the help of a book such as this one. Other helpful books and tapes are listed in the Further Resources section. Taking a class may help, though, especially when you're just starting out. If you decide to take a class, ask about the teacher's training and approach. Look for someone whose approach seems to mesh well with your goals and style as well as your family's values and beliefs. Your parents can help you make a good choice. Once you start the class, trust your instincts. If anything makes you feel uncomfortable, look for a new teacher. Remember that there are many, many forms of meditation. You don't have to feel locked in to one particular approach.

Question: Now that I'm meditating, can I stop going to counseling or taking my medicine?

Answer: No. As you've seen, meditation can have positive effects on your emotional and physical health. However, it is meant to be used along with standard counseling or medicine, not in place of such care. If you are being treated for an emotional or physical condition, talk to your counselor or doctor about the meditation you're doing. You'll probably get an encouraging response.

One last piece of advice: Be sure to enjoy your meditation practice. It should leave you feeling calm and relaxed yet alert. Meditation can help you develop your power of concentration. This power, in turn, can be used to develop your mind, body, and spirit. Meditation can also help you connect with yourself and others. In addition, it can bring you a sense of inner peace. When the outside world gets a little crazy, it's nice to know there's always an island of calm within.

Glossary

Buddhism: a major religion in Asia, which has a strong tradition of mindfulness meditation

contemplation: the act of reflecting on a certain experience, issue, or spiritual truth in an effort to gain greater insight into it

fight-or-flight response: the body's automatic reaction to any threat—real or imagined, physical or emotional

flow: the state in which you get so wrapped up in whatever you are doing that you lose yourself completely in the activity frontal lobe: part of the brain responsible for high-level mental functions; during meditation, this area is less active

Hinduism: the major religion of India, which has a strong tradition of mantra meditation and yoga

imagery meditation: the practice of focusing your mind on imagined sights, sounds, smells, tastes, or other sensations

insight meditation: a popular form of mindfulness meditation; also known as Vipassana meditation

limbic system: part of the brain that plays a key role in emotion, memory, and the regulation of heart and breathing rates; during meditation, activity in this area increases

lotus pose: a sitting position in which you sit cross-legged with a straight back

lovingkindness: a way of caring about yourself and others that can be strengthened through meditation and contemplation

mantra: a special word or sound that is repeated over and over meditation: the practice of focusing your mind on a particular thing or activity

mindfulness: the practicing of focusing your attention on whatever you are experiencing from moment to moment

om: a mantra that, in Hindu tradition, is believed to be the sound of the vibration of the universe

parietal lobe: part of the brain that processes information from the senses; during meditation, activity in this area slows down

relaxation response: a state of deep rest that reverses the physical and emotional effects of the fight-or-flight response

reticular formation: part of the brain that controls consciousness and arousal; during meditation, arousal signals are muted

self-awareness: the act of observing your own thoughts, feelings, and sensations t'ai chi: system of physical exercise that uses slow, flowing movements; traditionally, t'ai chi also uses special breathing and meditation techniques, which are thought to promote overall health

thalamus: part of the brain that relays information from the senses to other areas of the brain; during meditation, the flow of information is slowed

Transcendental Meditation (TM): a form of meditation in which the person focuses on a mantra

yoga: a system of physical exercise that uses special body postures to stretch, strengthen, and align the body; traditionally also is a system of mental discipline that includes meditation

Zen: a branch of Buddhism that stresses mindfulness meditation

Further Resources

Books

Gordhamer, Soren. *Just Say Om!* Avon, Mass.: Adams Media Corporation, 2001.
A book about meditation and mindfulness, it is geared to slightly older teenagers than the other books listed here.

Gregson, Susan R. *Stress Management*. Mankato, Minn.: Capstone Press, 2000.
A book about managing and reducing stress.

Hipp, Earl. *Fighting Invisible Tigers: A Stress Management Guide for Teens*. Rev. ed. Minneapolis: Free Spirit Publishing, 1995.
A book about identifying and coping with stress.

Sainte Croix, Judith. *Everything You Need to Know about Meditation*. New York: Rosen Publishing Group, 2002.
A book about meditation, which includes thirteen exercises to get you started.

Silas, Elizabeth, and Diane Goodney. *Yoga.* Danbury, Conn.: Franklin Watts, 2003.
This book includes step-by-step instructions for various yoga postures for beginners, as well as additional information about yoga.

Weiss, Stefanie Iris. *Everything You Need to Know about Yoga: An Introduction for Teens.* New York: Rosen Publishing Group, 1999.
A book about yoga, which includes a chapter on meditation.

Youngs, Bettie B., and Jennifer Leigh Youngs (eds.). *A Taste-Berry Teen's Guide to Managing the Stress and Pressures of Life.* Deerfield Beach, FL: Health Communications, 2001.
A book about handling stress that includes sections on breathing exercises, muscle relaxation, and imagery.

Audiotapes

Relaxation Exercises for Students: Tape 1. Boston: Mind/Body Medical Institute, 1995. A tape of imagery meditation exercises.
Relaxation Exercises for Students: Tape 2. Boston: Mind/Body Medical Institute, 1996. Includes exercises for breathing, muscle relaxation, and imagery meditation.

Videotapes

Meditation for Teens. Sacred Mesa Productions, 1998 (VHS). This videotape features a group of teenagers talking about meditation. It includes a relaxation exercise using imagery.

Online Sites and Organizations

Mind/Body Medical Institute
www.mbmi.org
This site provides information about stress and the relaxation response.

TeensHealth.org
www.teenshealth.org
This site offers advice about stress, which is geared especially to teenagers.

Index

About the Author

Linda Wasmer Andrews is a freelance writer from Albuquerque, New Mexico. She specializes in writing about health, psychology, and the mind/body connection. People often picture an author who writes about meditation as always cool, calm, and collected. Not this author. Linda works hard, gets stressed out, hates to sit still, and sometimes loses her temper. In short, she is someone who really *needs* to relax her body and calm her mind, and meditation is the best way she knows to do it. This is Linda's seventh book. In addition to writing full-time, she is currently completing a master's degree in health psychology through Capella University.

Acknowledgements

Many thanks to the following people, who kindly shared their deep knowledge of meditation with the author: Heather Sundberg, Family Program Manager, Spirit Rock Meditation Center, Woodacre, California; Jennifer Johnston, Education Initiative Codirector, Mind/Body Medical Institute, Boston, Massachusetts; and the students at the Maharishi School of the Age of Enlightenment, Fairfield, Iowa.